PARTICLES OF LIGHT

PARTICLES OF LIGHT

THE POETRY OF CHRIS M L BURLEIGH

POEMS, PUNS, WORD PLAY, AND WITTY ONE-LINERS

Matador
9 Priory Business Park,
Wistow Road, Kibworth Beauchamp,
Leicestershire. LE8 0RX
Tel: 0116 279 2299
Email: books@troubador.co.uk
Web: www.troubador.co.uk/matador
Twitter: @matadorbooks

ISBN 978 1788039 086

British Library Cataloguing in Publication Data.
A catalogue record for this book is available from the British Library.

Printed and bound in the UK by 4edge limited
Typeset in 11pt Minion Pro by Troubador Publishing Ltd, Leicester, UK

Matador is an imprint of Troubador Publishing Ltd

To everyone who has moved me
Through their life
And especially to my family
And wife.

ACKNOWLEDGEMENTS

Within 'Love is Blind'. The author wishes to thank the National Association for the Advancement of Colored People for authorizing the use of Dorothy Parker's work

CONTENTS

Reflective and Descriptive

Love Poems

Reflective and Descriptive

LANCASHIRE LASS

Annie alone
Confined within her square-stoned cottage
No callers come to stir the silence
Tea-time shadows move around a motionless room
A click-clock paces the passage of time.
Annie, sat, stare-careless
Glazed-gaze
As embers flush, cokes collapse,
Crunch in a glowing grate.
Slow sun slips
Spills flames across the limp land,
Skeletal trees stand, faint with frost.
A lattice window lit
Sill-stood,
Watches failing fires.

The Shipwreck
(28 sailors, 3rd February 1994)

Cradle cry, cling or die
Dinghy-dashed, (rescue by).
Spear of light piercing the night
Lance-lunged, plunged in Deep.
Wounded wave, writhe-wide
Back-curled crest
Furled, then swirled.
Lashed-by, wind-wound, whipped water
Spray-spat, flicked-face
Laced-neck
Soaked sop, mop-matted, hoar-hair
Salt-licked, white flecked.

Bucking bark, coffin craft, bell boat battered
Raised and rolled, tossed, then tolled
Hold!
Cold, let loose,
Lost.

Cavernous-wave-grave, deaths-in-depths.
Dark, darkness, downed, drowned.
No sight
No sigh
No sound.

Time Present

Parents passing.
These were their streets, stations
Sights
Small boy at their side
Learning London,
Now a visitor, business or pleasure
But what pain.
The past is present
Less than half remembered
Faint recollection
Felt association,
I reach, stretch, strain, scream
Yearning to connect
Events and situations
With extant locations
In one unity
Enduring Time.

Loss

Grief is such a cruel emotion,
It hits you with more than one wave,
And just when you think you've reached the shoreline, saved,
You find yourself still tossed in the immensity of an ocean.

Fox

Fox stretches over the road
Extends across my headlights.
Focused on the far hedge
Nose reaching for the shadow of the bushes
High, stiffened brush points back towards
The disappearing path as he leaves.
I watch, swerve, but in his single minded purpose
I am not there.

BLACKBIRD

Blackbird in a bush
Bead-eye, yellow beak
Red-round berry
Bright.
Bush hop
Frost-crisp web-twig
Leaf-twist, neck twitch
Bird flick
Dark dart
Gone.

ANNIE

Fading flames flicker from creaking coals,
Cokes collapse in a dying grate
Annie sits alone, thoughts gazing into a faltering
fire-dance.
Silence fills the glowing room,
A tick-tock paces the passage of time.
Outside, skeletal trees stand, faint with frost,
A weeping sun slips behind a weak horizon.
Annie, stare-careless
Waiting, watching fires.

Fit Child

In drizzling rain the headlamps dazzle me.
I am remote, distant,
And my hurting head blurs as I strain to see.
Mum struggles to wipe my face,
I shake my head
Trying to avoid her attentive hand.
Why are they fussing, why can't I stand?
I am too big to be picked up.

Now I am going upstairs, peering over a shoulder,
People are following me. It must be my family.
They are all looking at me, talking with words
Making no sense.

I am curled up, moving backwards.
They place me on my bed.
The bunk above is pressing down, containing me.
Someone leans in, following me into the blackness
Where I am lying.
The dark room closes in and the shadows I can sense
Are standing near, murmuring concerned sounds,
Who are they, and why are they there?
In a moment I am gone from them,
I am in a frenzy of dream-clips in shades of grey,
Touched here and there with flashes of dark green
And amber-yellow.

They are disturbing my frantic isolation.
In the still darkness, I cannot see who they are.
I am hot, sweating.
Somebody places a cold disc on my chest
Then again, then again.
I want to go back to my solitude and sleep.
The shadows are still there and I want to speak to them,
I cannot think what to say, and no sounds come from
my voice.
They are in the room, but not in my world,
Why haven't they all gone to bed?
I want them to comfort me, but I want them to go
And I want to go, to descend again
To the enormous chaos of my unconscious retreat.

I feel myself sinking backwards
Deep, deep into my mattress
And I see the shadows and the blackness
Sucked out of my view, leaving only a blank emptiness.
I do not try to understand. I stare into nothingness.
And I wish it was morning.

Winter Hills

Do you remember the long cold winters
We used to have,
Before climate change brought
Slow autumn
Unsurprising spring
And rash-red summers?
When snow fell early and froze,
And fell again, and again
Deepening, fresher with each fall,
Whiter on white?
We walked on the tops then
Each foot-fall disappearing
Into prints left by someone
Unseen ahead.
Hauling our boots
Heaving our stride into the next step,
Tiring lead-legs weighted,
Sky greying greyer the steeper we climbed.
We spoke little, breathlessly concentrating,
Our thoughts puffing into the frozen air.
We stood on those tops then,
Looked down through the late afternoon light
To the shy, silent town
Scarffed in silk,

Hiding in chiffon mist.
Hurrying down, running sideways
Our feet shaving the snow,
Scuffing, sliding, scattering spray
Where they fell.

Now the snow hardly settles at all,
No mystery winter world
Transforms these hills.
Families roam, run a dog
Wander, where we were young.

Remember we said
'Will we remember that cold
When we are old'.
Now, we are dead.

Angel of the North

Claw-cling
Earth-angel
Spread wing,
Sinews stretch, strain to stand
Withstand
North wind.

Pigeon Loft

Sit, coo,
Shit, poo,
Birds flew –
Bird flu?

Amnesty

Peace dove, caged, contained,
Clipped flight camera-caught.
Iron will, free thought
Barred, fenced, fought.
Garden gate ground-hop,
Flicker,
Stop.

Aubade

Electric pips peep into my sleeping
Half-heard poke that pushes at my dreams,
A blurred ceiling glows with rising time,
Mystery dawn still hides in misty coldness,
Not yet stretched, split its darkness,
No squint of day, cracking clinging night.

The street belongs to duty,
Singing bottles gonged on solid stones,
Dragged frost scratched, revealing,
Headlamps lit
Throated engine cleared
Dawn neared.

DIVIDED LOYALTIES

Alnwick Castle to Tintagel
Menai Straits to Dover,
Moray Firth to Land's End
I love this land, all over.
I've travelled in Europe and Africa,
This is the best land I have seen,
I uphold its values and traditions,
But I won't swear an oath to the Queen.

I'm Christian, not Church of England
So I'm, sort of right-religion,
But if I don't swear allegiance
Is that a disloyal decision?
Will you deny me freedom of conscience,
That most British freedom,
Do you make me a second-class citizen
If I don't want a United *Kingdom* ?

From Durham to York, Cambridge to Bath,
The Lakes, The Dales, Forests and Fens,
Folk songs, thatched cottages
Shingle beach or chalk down –
I love this beautiful island
But I won't swear an oath to the Crown.

A Tragedy

Narrator   No one heard her fall, or heard Natasha call
Dying alone in a boiling bath,
Her lover dead to her final cries,
With her life hanging by a thread
Her lifeline lies comatose on their lovers' bed.
She draws us, touches with those enticing eyes,
Her haunting beauty, intangible, vanished,
A life so full, now piteously denied.

Ipswich five, prostitute lives,
(Labels dissemble and disguise),
Sisters in streets, daughters, wives
Mothers giving love, by selling sex.
The highway home dogged by drag-net dealers
Paved with punters, tolled by pimps
Cluttered by we clamouring, uncaring crowds.

Rachel   'No one can say how I died
And neither can I tell,
Foetal-found, kneeling, curled on kitchen floor
Needle hanging in my arm.
Drugs, they really screw you up,
Dealers, men, they just screw you'.

Narrator   A lost lover hanging from a rope
The end of talent, promise, hope.
The pusher, the punter, the pimp

Chorus*   And the papers; * 'you hypocrites!
          Believe not what is written, what *they* say –

          I am your daughter, I am your wife,
          I am the one who gave you life.
          Coke or heroin, our lives are the same,
          Conceal our guilt and hide our shame.
          Pay them now and we all pay tomorrow
          In misery, desperation, despair, or sorrow.'

Natasha   'Look into my eyes, hold my hands
          Touch my sides,
          See I am alive!
          Know I am vital, vulnerable, frail and full
          I am loved, I loved, laughed, and cried,
          Know I lived, lived falteringly,
          And tried'.

SHOT AT TRAFALGAR

Tilt your head and shut one eye,
Spy Nelson in the sky.
Spring sun squints through hurrying clouds,
Fluted grey column stretching high,
Granite fountain firing rainbow spray,
Monochrome pigeons hopping, pecking
Bead eye watching, head-nod – checking,
A flurry of wings flapping in your face
Your smile flashing between the beats.
I want to catch you
Hold still,
While I snap you.

'Working late at the office'

Lady at her lonely latter-day loom
Lit by the light of her laptop,
Spinning thoughts into MS Word
Painting pictures to PowerPoint.
Fingertips dance on click-step keys
Poised pauses spring into cascading prose.
Her hair flows in Pre-Raphaelite waves
Glasses bright with the glow of words.

Solitary now as the office empties,
Alone with her evening of enforced overtime.

Forget-me-nots

Lady leaves without her lead,
Making for her meeting.
Sans umbilical, her laptop will soon die.
I cry, with a smile she returns and retrieves –
Power to bring her presentation to life.

When I'm Sixty-Four

When I'm sixty-four
It'll be just like being four:
I'll tip my chair
And fall out forwards,
Graze my knee, and not care
Like babies and cowards.
I'll have my own indoor climbing frame
To carry around as part of my game.
I'll chatter endlessly about nothing at all,
But be in my own world whenever you call.
I'll go to bed early, thoroughly tired out,
And still need the toilet in the middle of the night.

When I'm sixty-four
Will you bother anymore?
If I'm difficult and tetchy,
And my memory's sometimes sketchy,
If I lose my money and mobile,
If I become slow and feeble,
Will you tend me and care
For me, help me up the stair?
Will you love me, honour, cherish and obey
Just as you promised, seems like yesterday?

And when I'm sixty-five,
Will I still be alive?

LIFE

First
I was cosy
Then
I was cold.
When it was frosty
I froze.
Hot
And cold.
Life
That's the way it goes.

I'M BORED

Is there anything to do
At Sutton Hoo
The tired traveller wondered?
Can I see very much
Does it all say 'Do not touch'
The treasures tomb robbers hadn't plundered?

PHEASANT

Pheasant found
Garden ground
Runs his realm of lawn.
Neck bejewelled,
Cloaked in ripples of rust
And gold, and emerald.
Arrogant strutting
Neck jerks
Bead-eye knowing,
Watches the moment –
And is gone.

Fun and Games

A family album is going around,
Fingers pointing, turning the pages,
Acclamations at recollections.
She gazes wearily at faded photos:

A girl in the Forties
A black and white world,
A scruffy yard and broken fence,
Her dress tight-stretched across her knees,
She's straining to save a goal.
Detached from their poverty, all eyes on the ball,
Kids playing games, having fun.

Party bubbles of chatter, burst by her ears,
She does not hear,
Floating in thoughts
Barely engaged.

She sits, surrounded, weakly detached
Too tired to try
Too resigned to mind,
No games now.
This will be the final family fun.

BREAKING NEWS

Richard III
Got re-interred
But nobody heard.
A villain and a baddy
(According to history)
Dug up from under a parking lot
But some suicidal German Airwings pilot
Crashed his plane
(He must have been insane)
Spreading mayhem, wreckage, and carnage
To make his mad and grim message
(What was it he wanted to say
In that dramatic and dreadful way?)
He killed all the passengers and the crew
A tragedy for all who loved and knew.
No mortal remains, just body parts,
No funerals for grieving hearts,
Just painful memories of wasted lives –
Sons and daughters, husbands, wives.
These innocents lie scattered
As if their lives never mattered.
But a villain and a baddy
(According to history)
Got re-interred –
But nobody heard
Because of the breaking news
'bout those passengers and crews.

TO A POPPY

Defiant December poppy
Bent, lowed,
Lonely, determined,
Bold poppy!

Tormented, tortured,
Downpour-drowned, wind-wrecked.
Denying torrents and batterings,
The slenderest stem shaken by shuddering gusts,
Brave poppy!

Confused poppy, confounding seasons,
One patient bud prepared for this still day.
Pale-petalled, pathetic glow,
Proud poppy!

Raggéd poppy, ravished poppy,
Ripped and stripped,
Still clinging and springing
Against a wasting wind.

Farewell to Erossos

Sappho was a poetess
And I'm a poet too.

Stilted restaurants straddle sand and strand,
Reach along the stony beach.
Surge of early diners
Shuffled into party packs
Take seats and watch the dance of waves –
Tingling ripples juggling splinters of light,
The glow-slow sky over a silhouette hill.

Sappho was a poetess
And I'm a poet too.

Short-cropped women, hand in hand
Stumbling along the soft-sink sand,
Making for bars, pink and pastel blue,
(not for me but perhaps for you)
Taking spiritual nourishment at an abstract slab –
Female forms, nudes entwined
(I take people as I find).

Sappho was a poetess
And I'm a poet too.
When summer fun fades
And winter rains return,
When shops are shut
And restaurateurs rest,

Is Sappho still revered
As a classical poetess?

Sappho was a poetess
And I'm a poet too.

MATES

'Ere mate'! he cried, so they became,
Walking, slow stroll to school,
Talking, aimless chatter.

Parted at eleven, weekend wanderings,
Seeing the world through each other's eyes –
Worlds separated at schools' end.

Only he could be
The Best Man –
Marriage seemed not in his plan.
For years, chatter an annual letter.

The letter from his mother didn't explain –
Was it narcotics or alcoholics,
Women or men?
But Nick got sick
And quick
Took to his bed –
In the morning, found dead.

Drunken Disorderly

Today
I hit the bottle,
It smashed
And the message that came out
Really knocked me out.
Tomorrow
I'll get smashed.

Who goes there?

Winter walking
Wrap-up needed
Woolly hat headed,
Hunched and huddled
Warm coat cuddled
Garb-concealed; gait-revealed –
Definitely Daphne!

Rushing Raisa

Bearskin beauty
Russian fashion
Coat, cardigan, designer cut,
Face as snow.
Black boots dash
Dart eyes met,
A second yet,
Then go.

Ruby Wedding

Forty years – and it only feels like yesterday
Does it sometimes feel an eternity?
Time flies, and time stands still.
Take time to look back at the past,
Take your time enjoying every today.

Forty years – life begins at forty,
So many years still to enjoy.

From a Best Man
To the best couple ever –
Together forever – Gil and Di.

Motorway Hawk

Hawk hovering
Sunlit
Grey wing
Feather flickering
Blue sky flash
Still, dash
Watch, crash.

Maddy

Music flows from head to toes
As Maddy goes
Dancing.
Foot flings
Arm waves
Body sways
As Gay sings,
And drums beat to Maddy's feet.
Guitar screams and violin whines,
Lights dash across guitar flash,
Band one body
Spotlight on Maddy.
You're entranced –
Watch Maddy dance.

EVENING SHORE

Boom-waves pounding on a suffering shore
Solid-soaked, hard sand
Draw-sing, drag-cling,
Stone-rattle, retreating sea
Yawns wide in threat,
Reveals menacing magnitude,
Fresh-flung, relentless rhythm.

Lift eyes, blind look
A failing, far distance,
A dying sun, hollow, fire-frozen gaze
Stretches a flame-spread finger
Over the restless, slow-settle,
Chattering surface of the sea.

GOAT

Tethered goat
Thong-squeak, collar-creak,
Strains in his orbit,
Crunch-tears green grass.
Pitiful coat,
Neck bent, neck-nod
Tired gaze in a watery eye,
Wedded to this stake-ring,
Rounded wrenched,
His keeper comes
Uproot
Tug-target,
Stake-struck
Blind bull's-eye driven,
Stuck!

NIGHT FLIGHT

Night return,
Dazzle descend
A burst of brilliance
Bellies above a lit-strip runway,
Tip touch
Roll the long of landing,
Flight finished!

TRAMP

Railway waiting room
Tramp, buckled on a bench,
Bags of belongings picked from bins,
Blue coat greyed with grime,
Leathered face, weathered skin
Wrinkled brown,
Her wire hair rag-wrapped.
Journey's end.

———

In a moment
The beginning is at an end
And the end is just beginning –
In a moment.

CLOUDBURST

Water washes verdure
Runs down gullies, reaches lodge
Gushing, rushing
Swirls over pebbles, pours down stones
Swells and foams the whirl in the pool.

Beyond the river widens, forks and yawns
Sluggish and massive the hills roll back
Rise, climbing to the mist, clinging to clouds,
A moment revealed.

A STITCH IN TIME

Make me a jacket
Wear it fine,
Under cover
In the rain.

Stitch by stitch,
Wear it well,
Leave it loose
For casual.
And you're not as slow
As two can,
For there's none can sew
As you can.

Perfect Sense

Wind-bright clouds
Brushed by trees
Growing through a chasms of light,
Fragments flicker in pools below.

Somewhere between the light and the reflection,
Between the wind and the weather
In the shadow
Drifts perfection.

Cardiff Streets

Through rain and patter
Splash and muddy water
Flag-stones tripping
Down and puddles deepen,
Up and hidden
Dipping,
Wind-run clouds
Star shrouds
Catch the skies,
Stray-spray breeze
Stands, smoulders in trees
Gushes and dies.
When weather sprinkles, wind rushes to work,
Let me walk you through the dark.

———*vvv*———

A pirate moon
Slowly slips through clouds,
Rippled like tide marks
In the pale sand.

———*vvv*———

Through the stinging-chill air,
And stretched across a vertical horizon,
A frozen sheet of silver cloud
Snapped jagged,
Sings like frost on a tinted window pane.

———*vvv*———

A sick moon
Struggling through clumps of cloud
Tufted here and there
In the fen of night.

———*vvv*———

Poppy standing solus
Silent, brash rash-red
In a verge, waivers
Brushed by a rush of
Vehicles.
High summer
Soon dead.

———∿∿∿∿———

Poppy brash rash-red
Standing solus in a verge
Silent. Waivers
Brushed by a rush
Of vehicles.
Hi summer
Soon dead.

———∿∿∿∿———

Pale poppies still puncture
Bare wasteland
Though fast frost has claimed dying September,
Weeping under a bleeding sun,
Cry-bled spread crimson-gold on morning mist,
Pink-petal pathetic,
What point protest?

SUMMER SOLSTICE

Wooton lying low
Spread softly among wide-yawn fields,
Long mute slopes draw gentle breath.
A spire stretches to a pale-warm sky.
Treading lightly between sleeping graves,
Moving lives on leaning headstones.
The day stirs quietly between life
And death.

———

An autumn blast
Bursts up a passage,
Shocked shoppers
Stiffened shoulders,
Defend their coats,
Sudden honed
Like instant statues.
A confusion of leaves
Rushes into swirls around
Tree legs
Stick-steps...

Day-dry over
Treading night-foot,
Leaf-pulp, puddle-sog,
Submit and settle,
Village slips under a rain-sheet
Sprinkle cover.

FROST

Fingers of frost that signs the failing season
Low gold sun strains through glowing fog,
Breath of winter
Hushed on frozen fields.

Mind muffle-mumbled, thought depressed,
Faith found, confounded,
Beauty shed, life shred, decay spread,
Blinded, bled.

Dawn
Already dying
Daylight
Barely born
The moon-babe crying
A mist shroud,
Sky grey-weeping
Vague wraps
Fall sweeping,
Light-licks the skeleton trees,
Morning
In mourning.

Winter sun
Weak-warm, pale strength
Pushes shyly from behind wide clouds,
Timid-tints the countryside
Once brush,
Wipes a copper wash,
Welcome!

Wind-whip wave-freeze
Ice-edge, sculpture blown
Razor-hung.
Snow-shift, stuck-poise
Dry drift.

WINTERSCAPE

Wide-bright, dazzle-white
World-waste
Unrelenting
Sky-fused winterscape.
Ungiving ground
Cold-hard, rock-rut
Frozen.
Distant stick-snap trees
Still-stiff
Stuck silent
By a muffle-mist.
Opaque
Vague
Grey-pearled, frost-focus
Ice-marbled mirror,
Depth-hewn
Skim-lake,
A deadland freeze-bake.

THE SNOWMAN

Heavy tears drift down
In a night-grey sky
Snowman stands firm
Shows chill-cheer smile,
Chubby-shy.
Winter-dark, ice winds blow,
Snowman, weather-bear
A white-warm glow.
Watch him from your window,
He softly shines, lifted by your light.
Snowman, simply silent
Challenges the night.

Boy in a white shirt

Poses for photos, goes where told,
Positioned under a garden tree,
The sun in his eyes,
A child's prayer book in one hand,
A white ribbon ties his arm –
Caught in a single, black-and-white shot.
Our lives have wandered a colourful, confused trail,
Strolled and strayed
From that dimly recalled album image,
But still the lost boy,
Clutching prayers
And squinting at the sun.

End of the party

I hadn't noticed it getting so late,
I was playing in the garden
Having fun in the sun
When they called me in.
I didn't know it was time to go.
Then you were at the door
Waiting for me.
Hold my hand
On the way home.

—◈—

Drizzle-drab dull fall
On a grey-coat day,
Brush spray dead play
On a grieving pane.
Miserable morning,
Sudden sunny
Cloud-cleared afternoon,
Pheasants in a field,
Stretch shadow
Ridge and furrow
Hedge-shrugged, twig bush-bailed,
Field boundary buds
Waiting for warmth to bloom.

—⁓—

Leafy lane
Blossom-blush
Wind-stray
Wander way.
Soft sun shyly shines,
Swaying sky,
Droplets of lights
Filtered through filaments trees,
Spill from flicker-leaves
Splash among skipping shadows.
Spring-dawn
First-warm
Live again!

—⁓—

I wish I could weep to wash away my sorrows.
Muffled thought, muted talk
And failed feeling.
Words are not enough to say my sadness.
Blindness
Darkness, deep despair
And desperate isolation.
The warmth of human kindness
Is not there
For consolation.
Breath and death
Both desired, each admired
Neither sought.
Nought.
I am no-one
I am done.

———

Age wearies me
The burden of living
Bears down, weighs on me
Birth and bereavement
Rejection
Exploitation
And bereavement.
While I wait for death
Where is merriment?

———

Fine fantasy!
I am plunged in icy depths
Drowning in cold currents
Shivering, I reach for a warmer current passing
It flows from me, I am pulled away,
Everything I cared for is lost in rejection
Warmth wraps another.

Autumn falls
And winter waits to waste me more.
Black, black, and blackness,
Condemned, chained in my dungeon, despondent.
Despair and desolation,
All hope extinguished,
Hollowed from my core.
All light disappears
And day all turned to darkness.

All that, is at an end,
All that is, at an end.
No more beginnings.

Years disappear,
We Spring alive,
I survive, I survive.

Love Poems

Single Rose

For you,
A single rose,
I chose,
I choose.

For you
I chose
A single rose.
I choose.

For you
I chose.
A single rose
I choose.

A single rose
I chose.
For you I choose.

ONE-NIGHT STAND

Star-bright
Travel light
Spend the night
With me.

Flutter-moth
Gentle, soft,
Dance
And flicker
Free.

THE BORDELLO

Stair-well lifting to the light,
Lady lead in your flight,
Landing-linger, stared-eyes met,
Vacant possession –
Love to let.

On my wedding day

After life comes death
And through death, new life
After-life.
  To my wife
  I leave my life
  As a wreath
  After death.
Through death comes new life.

The Triangle

I exist in two worlds,
I am in two minds,
And now I think
In two hearts
Too.

And this
Will break
Three hearts
In two.

Love in Old Age

You were nice to have
Warm to hold,
Too soon broken
Too soon old.

Last Will and Testament

I want to go into my autumn and winter
Reconciled to my God,
To my family,
To my wife,
And to my life.

—*vv*—

Lady, why look so sad?
All eyes are on you.
Lady, all about you woman.
Image held in mind's eye.
Woman, were I free,
Lady, leave me!

Dear [whoever], thanks for the letter,
It was really nice.
Thanks for breaking the ice:
Now, things can only get better.

A Londoner's Lament

You are gorn,
And I am left forlorn!

Une vignette

Ma Claire, il est claire,
Je vois, que tu ne m'aime assez,
Je crois, c'est parceque je suis plus agé,
Je sais, après ce soir, le désespoir

—◊—

Enfin j'accepte que personne ne m'aime
Sauf mon amie seule, ma femme.

School Boy Love

The hair, her hair!
I look, I stare,
But do not dare.
Pure poetry flowing,
All fantasy, knowing,
Science fiction doesn't compare.

Please don't yell,
Please don't tell.
Only see me, after the bell.

—~~—

Oh what a performance-
You dented my confidence,
Damaged my pride.
I shall go away and hide.

THE PARTING

No goodbyes
No rants, no insults
To shield our grief
No words of rage
No compliments to comfort
Or promises to 'speak again'.
No cruelly crafted selfish explanation
No tender words to soothe the pain of parting.

Wherever you are
Think of me.
Whatever you are doing
Picture me.
Whoever you are with
Remember me.
I really cared for you.

Cornered in a railway carriage, wedged
Raised newspaper, read
Newsprint mars your work-worn hands,
Tired shadows, limp-lights, mark age-waste wrinkles.
I, a platform-passer-by
Seek a contrary compartment.
Towed the same tracks, contained,
Our train, curtailed, a tunnel of light,
Truncated
Pushes out through a premature night.

Hills are erased
The background a haze
Of showers
Through spotted rain
On a window pane.

You are gone, erased,
And my passion ablaze
Like flowers
Diffused in myriad rows,
A single rose.

Though my tears are beaten
I still suffer the burden,
Always the pain,
A blood stain.

My love flows in its moods
Swells, its passion in flood,
Drains in pools of red
Springs and moistens my pulse of emotion
Congeals and scars,
Is healed by the tide of her tears.

She flows in moods and movements,
Swells and bursts, rises more
And drains in pools of red,
Overspills her passion in flood
Swirls and gushes and gentle falls,
Springs and pulses, stagnates and scars,
Breaks and heals by a tide of tears.

She tames the darkness when I stay,
Keeps the creeping loneliness at bay.

Defining Elements

You lie before the iron alter rail
Flanked by flaming sentry acolytes,
Their lights a sign of hope you live again.
In fire I see the light, the laughter of your eyes,
The warmth and wisdom of your enlivened face.

I stand beside you now with my silent grief
And contemplate the alchemy of our years.
The brass plate says so little, and says all,
Your name, dates, mother, wife recalled.
We stood here once before
And slipped our rings of gold onto our hands,
So vowed our lives together evermore.

A hillside family grave will be your home,
We family around the sodden mounds of earth.
Black brollies resist persistent Pennine rain,
Shaken, holding firm, in shuddering wind.
In the whistles and whines I hear you play again
The shrills and lows of your ebony clarinet.
I watch you go, descend into that void,
I cast a clump of soil, wait for all to go.

These are the elements of you –
This is the woman I knew.

Over the Moon

If Bob Dylan was right –
Love is but a four-letter word
What then did Elizabeth Barrett Browning
Really mean to ask?
'How shall I fuck you?
Let me count the ways.' ?
A Victorian sex manual
Subverted by sentiment and sensibilities?
It's Love that makes the World go round
So do wars and hatred
Slow Earth's rotation?
Then did the world spin faster in the Summer of Love?
Would Time pass quicker if lovemaking were our pass-
time?
'All you need is love'
'You are my world, you are my only love'.
The moon makes Earth wobble, creates the seasons
The moon turns the tide of our love.
'Fly me to the moon'
But let's not stop there
Onward with swift-footed feet to pink-flushed Mars
Then an arrow-shot rocket to velvet Venus
(Now, what could I possibly rhyme with 'Venus'? –
Don't even go there!)
Soar instead past Saturn's satin rings
Far from the furnace of our love –
To the Stars!

Swimming in azure galaxy seas
Rising on plumes of orange and green
Puffing purple, billowing blue
(Notice no mention of 'milky ways')
Holding hands, flying, floating, drifting
Swirling in clouds of pulsating gems
Our eyes are dazzled, we hold our breath
Climbing, diving.

Kaleidoscope debris, turning, churning
Fountains of fragments, needles of light
Flashes of shards pierce the night.

Telescoped vision
Magnified mission
Sated ambition
Succumbed, submission.
Surfing a chromatic arc of emotion
Colours diffusing, brilliance confusing
(Resist all references to 're-entry')
Softly descending, slowly returning
Gently landing
Back in time
Back in Time.
Our love is not a waste of time
We have both World enough and Time.
We can go a-roving by the light of the moon.

Our love was written in the stars
Our love is really down-to-earth.
In truth, Dylan was right –
Love is earthy.

Wit 'n Word

THE WORKING WEEK

Monday is none-day,
Tuesday is like two days,
Wednesday's will-it-ever-end-day,
Thursday is the day,
And Friday, I-am-free-day.

—⁓—

I have found
I cannot forget you
I cannot let you go.
A part of you
Is in me,
Though
It should be
The other way round.

—⁓—

Clothes maketh the man,
But lingerie maketh a woman.

—◦◦◦—

A God
Is a man's
Best fiend.

—◦◦◦—

Passion burns and burns out,
But true love goes on smouldering.

Pinnacles of Thought

The mountains of my mind
Are clouded in mist,
When it lifts
I shall rise to their summits.

Time-less

Eternity
Has no time
For chronology.

A Football Square

I have absolutely no interest in football –
I wouldn't know one end of a football
From the other.

———

A bowlful of mu-esli
Will help you poo easily.

———

Am I in Heaven or Hell –
I cannot tell.

—◦◦—

Architect
More artist than engineer,
Less businessman, than bohemian.

—◦◦—

Polly Rock
You knock
Me off
My perch.
I'm all a-quiver –
You're a knockout bird!

—◦◦—

If No Nude's
Undressed
Then No Nude's
Undone.

Drake
Spake
Hum
Drum.

HOPE

Hope springs eternal
In a young man's
Groin.

MORNING SEX

Sex in the morning
Sets a man up right
For the rest of the day.

Viagra man

Sex in the morning
Sets a man up-right
For the rest of the day.

What a way to go

He died with a smile on his face –
He took his own wife.

Marriage Vows

If I'm a raging bull,
Are you the red rag,
Or shall I just call you a cow?

More or Less Law-and-Order

Police,
Pl-ease police our streets
More,
And our motorways
Less.

Spring Time

To keep your garden
From dandelion clocks,
You have to keep
A dandelion watch.

Exotic Travel

Travel broadens
The bowel.

Fatal Attraction

Compelling, capricious, corpulent
Don't fall into the arms
Of the *femme fauteuil.*

Blown Away

In summer I go windsurfing
Winter is for 'mindsurfing'.
My mind is made up
I'll wind up
Making up poetry –
Unless the wind's up.

—⁓—

If music be the food of love
Do those who are tone deaf
Have no sexual appetite?

I used to be a paperboy –
Now I'm an adult cardboard cut-out.

GLOBAL CREDIT CRUNCH

Re-possession is nine-tenths
Of the poor.

CHARITY ENVELOPES

Excuses, refusals, and empty envelopes returned,
Mean-mindedness makes me so angry –
I hope these refusniks never need charity.

RISING PRICE OF PETROL

The car in front
Is a toy motor.

Lack of Libido

It's no good putting on that outfit –
I can't do anything about it.

US Presidential Prediction 2008 (McCain/Palin)

You ordered
oven chips
But you got
Half-baked Alaska.

Think before you buy

A God is for Afterlife –
Not just for Christmas.

Suburban Scandal

Among the expected corruption
Of middle-class Autumn gardens,
Among the silent, majority shrubberies
They unearthed a particular scandal,
And called it 'Squeaky gate'.

Neither PC nor WC

If a woman tells you she has diarrhoea
Pinch her bottom.
If that doesn't work
Give her a tap on the behind.

(Bit of) Rough Justice

Payment for sex
Is to be an offence –
And this will be enforced
By on-the-spot fines.

A New Watch?

Contemporary designs may soon be out of date,
But my old watch is time-less.

More *money*, than *cents*

Some women
Have more money
Than dress sense.

―∿―

I used to be
An Angry Young Man –
I'm still angry! [this line to be performed like a grumpy
old man].

Ever Hopeful

An optimist is always hoping for more sex
And a pessimist doesn't know when he's had it.

Negative Reporting

'No news is good news'
But in the British Press
No news is **good** news.

Marriage

She's she,
I'm me –
And ne'er the twain shall meet.

Sweet Multiplication

Three Twirls are thirty Twix.

Nothing to lose?

A well-made smoothie
Will pass straight through me

British Election 2010
(after the death of Eric Segal)

Love is
Never having to say
You're Tory.

The lesser of evils

While single
You can always have sex,
But once married
You're really fucked.

Bare with me

In the US citizens have a right
To bear arms,
But in some countries they don't even have a right
To bare legs.

LOVE IS BLIND
OR, BEAUTY IS IN THE EYE...

'Men seldom make passes
At girls who wear glasses',
But men go into frenzies
Over women wearing contact lenses.

AN ACCOUNT OF LOVE

Shall I reduce you to a coin I toss,
Heads I gain, tail's a loss?
You are worth much more than this.
If luck has linked our lives together
Will Fortune's spin steal back your treasure,
One ill wind slam shut the door
By which, once made rich, now poor,
Not caring what I shall miss?
Gold sovereign-sunlight gilds the darkest day
Moon's silver pieces spill an argent light.
Your interest drives my sombre moods away
Words that wet the driest drought of night.
Strange lady, why do you tax me this way?
I am spent. I have nothing more to say.

Whatever turns you on

Clothes maketh the man
But lingerie maketh a woman.
The widest choice is M&S
But really, hardly S&M.
John Lewis caters for the functional fit,
Mechanical, supporting, but boringly dull kit.
La Contessa is more frills and lace
For the fuller bust – rather in your face.
The Ann Summers range
Is alright for a change,
But personally I prefer
Agent Provocateur.

High-rise city non-sense

Up on the roof
You could touch the sky
But here on the ground
It's low-light, and all sound.

H1N1

I feel so bad
I just want to die,
But if dying's any worse than this
It's going to be murder.

No regrets

If I could have my time over again
I would…

Lottery Win

A fool and his money
Are soon outed.

i LOVE

u
r
the Apple
of my
i

NO FLIES ON HIM

Once – bitten.
Twice – fleas.

LITTLE GIRL'S HOLIDAY SOUVENIR

Fans for the memory.

THE POWER OF WORDS

Fencers swear
By the S-word.

Speak for yourself!

'A sexagenarian'
Has nothing to do with 'sex'.

I need a break

I must sit down
For some
'Phew' moments.

Sexual orientation

A pessimist thinks the best is behind him
While an optimist thinks the best is still to cum.

No fool...

This old yoghurt
Is really
Set in its whey.

Dining out

Dinner was heavy
But lunch was a walk in the park.

Cheek by jowl

Our neighbour Sue
Is doing a poo
I can hear through
Their loo
Window
You know.

Fantasy Knowledge

Using Wikipedia
Is having your head
In The Cloud.

Cheques and balances

Internet dating
Is a kind of
On-line bonking.

(Spend a) penny for your thoughts

If we had two sticks
We could play pooh-sticks.
And if we had three sticks
We could play wee-sticks.

Just in time

With thyme on your hands
You have thyme to clean up.

Best Dressed

If you are going
Dressed as you are
Then I'll go
Dressed,
As you are.

I'm Game

Is this the right time of year
To shoot a deer?
You couldn't use your 12-bore
To bring down a wild boar,
Though you would use a cartridge
To knock off a partridge.
It would be rather pleasant
To dine on pheasant,
But to bag a duck
Demands speed and pluck,
And you need plenty of nouse
To pick off a grouse,
But you only need a smidgin
To catch a pigeon.
Game over!

Trojan Horse

Beware Geeks
Bearing gifs.

Sounding off

Country walk,
Shriek of pheasant in a field
Lying fallow.
Lying fellow –
He should squawk!

C'est La Vie

I got a terminal diagnosis
Today.
Oh well,
That's the way
Life goes.

Rare Bird

Once Bitten,
Now shy.

I'll drink to that

Vino veritas –
Message in a bottle.

Colonial Power

Once a great colonial power,
Its Power now in the hands
Of a foreign power.

Hell and Damnation

Damned if I do
Damned if I don't –
Then I'm damned if I will!

I must fly

Time Flies
Around my head.
Sense of decay.
One minute
I'm alive,
The next
Dead.

Midday Menu

A hot soup bowl,
A ham and cheese roll,
An apple to crunch –
Lunch!

———〜〜〜———

You are the cause
And the cure.

They always say
He's so good-lucking
In his beau-tie
And dee-jay.

—◆◆◆—

Marriage is like sex itself –
Lots of ups and downs.

—◆◆◆—

You tell me you no longer
Have a partner –
Perhaps I could fill
That gap.

So you don't want sex with me?
Well then – fuck you.

ADVICE TO YOUNG MEN

When in a hole –
Keep pushing.

————

Even if we
Were [ever] Lovers
You would still be
Mistress of your life.

————

She sold him some software,
He gave her some hardware.

———∿∿∿———

What a lot of bozos –
They don't know their arses from their elbows!

———∿∿∿———

I'm not looking for a reply,
That would be
A bad idée
For both you and I.

———∿∿∿———

The attached belong to you.
They are crap
But all I could do.

Maxim

If you can't [really] write,
Rhyme.

Nursery Matters

Mrs Mac
Won't be back
For giving a smack
She's been given the sack.

Pride comes before...

A once skilled climber,
Now, a once killed climber.

No Time like the Present

The Past
Is always Present
And the Future
Does not exist.

Bad Shot

If I'd a gun
I'd put it to my head,
But I've none,
Else, by now I'd be dead!

ABOUT THE AUTHOR

Chris M L Burleigh grew up in South London, and read English at Cardiff. He worked in IT. Chris has been writing poetry since his teens, and has been a prizewinner with, and been published by, Fish Publishing. Chris is married, with three daughters, and four grandchildren.